Alfred Allnut

The Day-Star Prophet

Alfred Allnut

The Day-Star Prophet

ISBN/EAN: 9783337028312

Printed in Europe, USA, Canada, Australia, Japan

Cover: Foto ©ninafisch / pixelio.de

More available books at **www.hansebooks.com**

THE DAY-STAR PROPHET.

BY

MRS. ALFRED ALLNUTT.

LONDON:
HURST AND BLACKETT, PUBLISHERS,
13, GREAT MARLBOROUGH STREET.
1865.

The right of translation is reserved.

LONDON:
SAVILL AND EDWARDS, PRINTERS, CHANDOS STREET,
COVENT GARDEN.

TO THE

BLESSED MEMORY

OF

JOHN THE BAPTIST

THIS LITTLE POEM

IS REVERENTLY AND LOVINGLY

Inscribed.

CONTENTS.

	PAGE
THE ADVENT	3
THE PREPARATION	31
THE VOCATION	55
THE MARTYRDOM	77

The Advent.

"Thy prayer is heard! and thy wife Elizabeth shall bear thee a son, and thou shalt call his name John!" *Luke* i. 13.

The Advent.

HEY are old,
   The two who wander there,
   Drinking clear draughts of scented
      mountain air,
Ere yet the Evening's breeze hath sighed farewell
To the last gleam of gold
That pales and dies, touched by Night's shadowy spell.
And yet a glow,
Beyond the glow of youth, hath gemmed their eyes
Up-cast with martyr-rapture to the skies:
Such as perchance was kindled by the sight
Of Canaan's land, vouchsafed on Pisgah's height,
In his who ne'er within its bounds might go,
But who beheld it,—and was satisfied;
Beheld the goodly land,—gave thanks, and—died.

A calm and holy glow
Such as reflects the peace they, and they only, know,
Who having woo'd some Hope, with passionate desire,
Have watched it, murmurless, but sad, expire:
Who having wept it forth in burning tears,
And wrestled for it in strong cries and prayers,
Have listened to God's voice that answered—No!
And silent at His feet have let it go!
This they have done, the two who pause serene
To gaze upon the Landscape's sunset scene,
And read the message of its Maker's Love
Writ in the waves of the sky tide above,
As in a golden mirror glassing Heaven!

To them the foretaste of a joy was given,
Yet undefined! and had you asked them why
Their beaming eye shone forth their ecstasy,
They had not found reply.
For we can feel,
(We, living mysteries! who lost such light
When Adam hid among the Eden-glooms,
That now, a thousand forms elude our sight
This side our Tombs,
That else had brought us weel),

Yes, we can feel, what yet hath learned no word
To whisper of its being, scarce begun;
Can feel our deep heart's fibres thrilled and stirred
By **Heaven's choirs, albeit** all unheard;
For mighty joys, when shaping for the birth,
Vibrate with dawning **life,** the expectant One
Who shall receive them, — ere they reach **the**
    earth!

He is a Priest, the venerable man,
And Zacharias named, and she, his **wife**
Elizabeth, hath shared, **as** woman can,
The chequer'd joy and grief that made **his life.**
Their home is lowly, nestled 'mong the hills,
Yet shadowed by some grand o'ertowering Palm
Among whose branches Angels fold their wings,
Whispering **of** Heaven, when the air is calm.
But most, to minister those Angels love
To the aged Pilgrims, whose lone dwelling-place
Is here; shining so radiant, with the grace
Of righteous walk, and humble worshipping,
And steadfast faith. Of such the Angels sing
Memorials in the Palace of their King
When they return above.

THE ADVENT.

Thrice blessed Pair!
May we the rapture share
That lights your eye, but hushes all your tongue;
For we will stir your silence, with the breath
Of our warm sympathy, until its tide
Breaks into ripples, sways our hearts with yours,
And we together glide
Into the same sweet current,
Over which, the Bow of Promise hung
By God's own Hands,
Our onward progress spans!

The Priest hath deeper musings, more sublime
Aspirings, than the wife,
Though both weighed anchor, and set Thought afloat
From the same moorings on the coast of Life,
To which fond Memory had steered the boat
A backward course, through Time.
A glittering spot! where first the Sun of Love
Broke on their Lives, filling them all with light;
Broke as a revelation from Above,
And taught all things a fresh significance;
While thousand forms burst on their gladdened sight,
Undreamed of heretofore!—a new born sense

Showed all things changed **to joy**; but chief, displayed
Each to the other, glorified,—and made
Conformable **to the Ideal**,—dawning
Upon their **hearts, waked up,** in Love's young
    Morning.
Then they recalled
How calmer joy, **but not less joyful,** came,
And a great Hope, **they dared at last** to name
To God, and to each other;
" Oh, that Elizabeth **might be a mother!**"
At first they prayed **together, and were glad,**
Waiting a token **that their prayer was heard**;
And then, more earnest, but apart, **the word**
Of strong entreaty rose to listening **Heaven,**
And still no son was given,
And even Hope grew sad!
Yet still they asked, each curtaining the prayer
Within **the folds of** Darkness, **winging it with**
    tears
From solitary spots, the wife to spare
Her loved one,—he, his wife,—the double pain
Of a reflected disappointment;—fain
To believe the other had forgot
The Hope that was;—the Blessing that was not!

THE ADVENT.

Thus far they mused alike,—the Man receiving
What was—God's **Making**,—and at once believing
Had it been well, He had bestowed a Son,
Bowed humbly, and exclaimed—" His Will be done!"
And in Submission's valley plumed his wing
For the pure flight of lofty worshipping.

But, woman-like, the woman lingered on
Beside the grave, where lay dead Hope—so wan,
Musing, as one who muses in a dream
Of what is not—and of what might have been.

She loved her Husband, with the loyal love
Of a true Woman, true to God above,
True to herself, and therefore true to One
Whom God's uniting made, not hers alone,
But her,—her very self,—in mystic type
Of the great Marriage, which when Time is ripe
For God to give
The Nuptial Benediction, shall unite
The holy Church, enrobed in shining white,
To Christ the priestly spouse, thenceforth to live
One, in one home, for ever!

Well she knew
How deep and constant was the love he gave
In sweet exchange for hers. He was so true,
So gentle! Yet at times, austere and grave,
He awed her; and thus awed, she loved him
    more.
For Woman's love grows not beside the Man's
Like a young Palm, beside another Palm,
Growth answering growth, each self-sustained and
    calm,
But as a climbing plant, strong only in the strength
It leans on, when it spans
A sturdy stem, uptwining to the top,
Hiding the sterner outline of its prop
With gay festoons, and many a glowing length
Of linkéd flowers!

So she joyed to prove
That he had thoughts in which she bore no
    part,
Because it showed him great, and gave her heart
A sheltering sense of lofty strength, and still
Beckoned her onward Nature to fulfil,
From higher spheres, its destiny of love.

THE ADVENT.

And yet her love brought echoes back of pain,
For her poor heart, so satisfied with all
He was oft chafed itself, in secret thrall
Of power circumscribed, to be again
What she desired to him; and longed and sighed
For small endearments, he had not denied
Except as deemed unworthy of such love,
Such trust as theirs, which even in the proof
Were injured, being held needing proof.
Oh, she had never known this heart's lorn strife,
Had God endowed her with a child's young life
To live for—For to Babes men lavish throw
A thousand little fruits that bloom and grow
On fair Affection's boughs, which the Babe takes,
And, smiling at, forgets, or flings away;
But which his mother, gathering up, holds dear
For the hand's sake
That plucked them, and will lay
To ripen in the sunlight warm and clear
Of loving memory, to feast on with delight
Many days after.

    Then thought wandered on,
And, leaving Self behind, only beheld

THE ADVENT.

The warm and breathing image of a Son
With infant beauty filling all her home
And all her heart; till her aspirings swelled
To a Hope come
Of higher inspiration than her own.
The Jewish Matrons not for Sons alone
Asked with the fervour of a woman's prayer,
They sighed to welcome David's royal heir,
To guide the baby footsteps that one day
Should tread the earth in Universal sway,
And press to trembling lips the dimpled hand
Destined to wield the sceptre of their Land.
Then Love might lose itself in worshipping,
And captive Zion might behold her King;
And, rising from the chains that thralled her now,
Place her bright diadem upon His brow!
Oh, glorious hope! th' exultant spirit soared
In rapturous entreaty, come, great Lord!
Come even now, Desire of every Nation!
And bow all hearts in blissful adoration!
Come not to me, to glad an humble home,
But to thine Israel,—to all Nations come!
Elizabeth thus gained the lofty height
Her priestly spouse more quickly had attained.

He soared direct, as with an angel's flight,
While she the same pure elevation gained
In devious climb and weary pilgrim tread;
Both led,
By the same guiding, to one holy rest—
Both destined in one Blessing to be Blest.

And hence the joy that glittered in their eyes
Upturned with martyr-rapture to the skies,
Where the great coming Blessing, yet untold,
Hung o'er them like a Canopy of Gold
By angel hands upborne, whose burnished light
Thrilled in their hearts, though hidden from their sight.

Nature's great lamp hath flickered out and died,
And darkness falls upon the mountain side:
Homewards in peace the Pilgrims' steps are turning,
Within their breasts a pure Shechina burning,
Shut in with night and silence; as the veil
Before the Holy Place conceals the light
Of God's resplendent Presence, lest the sight
Should blast the curious eye, too rash, too frail.

THE ADVENT.

To-morrow morn the opening eye of day
Must see them starting on their steadfast way
To the fair Temple crowning Zion's height.

  They are come to the Temple
   Of gladness and song!
  Its colonnades ample
   The echoes prolong;
  Up the heights, streaming,
   Thousands are there,
  Every eye gleaming
   The worship to share;
  Every heart bounding
   With high hope and love;
  Every tongue sounding
   Its pæan above;
  Banners unfolding,
   The standards display,
  Of the tribes that are holding
   Their congress to-day;
  A mighty assembling
   Of bondmen and free,
  Mostly resembling
   The crowd that shall be

> Brought from all nations
>   When God shall appear,
> Each in their stations
>   His judgment to hear.
> The trumpets are sounding
>   In silvery strain,
> The priests are surrounding
>   The Altar again;
> Prostrate and lowly,
>   Respond as they sing,
> One God, ever Holy,
>   Of Israel is King!

Elizabeth within the court hath stayed,
Where, long ago, the childless Hannah prayed,
Unheeding all the multitude around—
Her soul with God alone, as his was found
Sleeping below the Ladder angels trod,
The golden Ladder to the house of God;
And to her trancéd soul a dream is given
Which makes that outer court "the Gate of
    Heaven."
Meanwhile her husband mid the Levites stands,
His silver trumpet silent in his hands,

THE ADVENT.

And while the tide of music ebbs away,
The lot is cast! Whom will God choose to-day
From the gold altar privileged to wing
In wreathing clouds the Incense offering?
The lot is cast! and Zachariah's name
Bursts from a thousand tongues with loud acclaim.
Then silence on the shouting thousands fell,
Worked by some mighty, all-pervading spell.
Meekly bowed down each Levite's reverend head—
God had passed by. "Thy Will be done," they said.
But lowliest his was bowed on whom the crown
Of God's acceptance rested, as crushed down
With overwhelming honour!

      Priestly hands
Drew back the curtains of the sacred place,
Which closed, and hid the Levite from the ken
Of all besides his Brethren;
And no trace
Upon their massive folds of broidery rare,
Remained to show that One had entered there.
Still were they vainly questioned by the eyes
Of thousand waiting worshippers around,
While on the outer silence fell the sound

THE ADVENT.

Of dim retreating footsteps. So the skies
Smile unresponsive in unruffled blue,
What time the tear-stained eye of parting Love
Its Heaven-ascending treasure would pursue,
To catch a distant glimmer from above,
Escaping from the opening Glory-gate!
Yet many a heart went with him as he trod
Through draperied shadows of the courts **of God**,
Still gliding onward in his robes of white,
Led to the Golden Altar by the light,
Already paling for its evening oil,
Of starry flame that crowned **with blossomy
   grace**
The seven-branched **lamp before the Holiest
   Place.**

A pause ensued for silent worshipping—
Then the soft perfume of the Incense stole,
Borne by the balmy breeze's fluttering wing
To those without, unto the weary soul,
Typing the Peace prayer brings, apart
From granted wishes, to the praying heart.
A longer pause, and then a rustling sound
Of expectation, as the groups around

Glanced eager on the yet unlifted veil,
The Priest's return to bless intent to hail.
Yet still he tarried! and the questioning eyes
Turned doubtful to the quickly dark'ning skies.
"He comes not," murmuring passed from tongue to
 tongue,
And Fear upon the crowd her shadow flung,
As each would read in other's awe-blanched face
The pending mystery of the Holy Place!
And still a further pause when words had died,
And the slow ebbing of Time's mighty tide
Was measured by the throb of anxious hearts,—
When lo! the curtain parts!
The Priest is come!
He waves a benediction from his hands,
Yet silent stands
Struck dumb!
And whispering voices swift the tidings spread,
That he had seen an angel!

The spangled veil of night fell gently round,
Hiding the marble temple's columned grace,
Hushing the tide of life, till every sound
Of man had ceased within the Holy Place.

THE ADVENT.

Only the wind sighed in the **deepened gloom**
Where late a thousand heaven-tuned voices sung;
Only the weary Bird, with quivering plume,
Sank with a twitter on her callow young.

On Zion's hill **the peaceful** moonlight slept,
Whence, spirit-like, it conjured phantom lights
Of weird shape, like sentinels that kept
Unmoved and silent watch upon the **heights,**
Starting from shadowy gulfs, like yawning tombs,
Till day's first beams **revealed them only towers**
Of rugged **rock, and** showed their grave-like
    glooms
But cradle-beds for perfume-breathing flowers.

Far stretching round, the slumbering city lay;
Its dream-led children wandering in repose
Through scenes impossible to waking day,
Too soon to call them back to work and woes!
Legion, the visions of the thousand eyes
Now closed in sleep, from where the Monarch lies
In purple state, to where the outcast child,
Dreaming of home and **love,** in sleep has smiled
A smile unknown to daylight!

THE ADVENT.

                    But no dream
Is found so fair as is the waking joy
Elizabeth hath gathered from the gleam
Of her mute husband's heaven-lighted eye.
To her there was no night:
Had not an angel spoke,
And filled her soul with light
Which overflowed her being like a tide
Before whose flood all barriers were broke,
While still it spread for ever far and wide,
And welling upward to the spangled dome
Arching our race's universal home,
Destroyed the bounds of Time, and rushing on
Like waters to the sea,
Or sunbeams to the sun,
Time to Eternity,
Made Heaven and Earth seem one?

She said no words of praise; words were too small
To chariot all her joy. Her heart was all
Aglow with praise, and like the Prophet's car
Of rushing flame, and fiery horses driven
By God's own hand beyond the utmost star,
Sprang silent into Heaven!

THE ADVENT.

The hope of years, how **soon to** be fulfilled!
"Elizabeth, thy wife, shall **bear a son!**"
Nor this alone with **joy her bosom thrilled,**
    And urged her prayer—" My God, Thy Will be
        done!"
That prayer which but **a few short hours before**
Had been the sigh of meek submission, now
The eager song of a heart welling o'er
With bright anticipation. **They were one;**
The sigh had tuned the song. **She who** could bow
Unmurmuring to be refused the boon
Her heart so longed to gain, could use **the joy**
Of granted prayer, and give God all the praise.
Thus deals **our heavenly** Father with the hearts
That He would gladden. **Thus He oft delays**
The Blessing **sought.** In darkness we crave light,
And first must grope our way through thicker night;
In mortal life, **for immortality,**
And death with spectral sceptre strikes **us down.**
Patience, then Hope; it is the way **which He,**
The Christ, hath trod—the cross **precedes the crown.**

"Elizabeth, thy wife, shall bear a **son!**"
This were such joy as other mothers knew.

Oh, mystery of love! each little one
Reveals delight undreamed of, **ever new**
Even to the latest mother Time shall bless,
As it was new to Eve!—a Babe's caress
Transforms all being! But had this been **all**
Elizabeth should know, no Angel's wing
Had waved adieu to Heaven the **news to bring,**
And bid it fall
Like an anointing oil, making **all**
Her future life a consecrated thing.

Listen again
The sacred **import of the** Angel's **strain!**

Not his own harp, **though** tuned to glorious themes,
Now vibrated to Gabriel's glowing hand;
Even amid the Temple's hallowed scenes,
The melodies of Heaven had been unscanned
By mortal sense. The Harp of Prophecy
Had **long been silent.** One by one
The olden **Prophets were inspired to try**
Its sounding chords, and **when** their task was done

THE ADVENT.

They had passed onward, mid the spirit-throng
To wait the purport of their shadowy song.
Last of the Seers, Malachi had died;
And since his day, no other hand had tried
The triple chord of prayer, and faith, and praise,
Till the far Future singing in God's hand,
Echoed the notes, in dim prophetic lays,
And soothed the sadness of a captive land,
And captive souls, with promised liberty;
Till Now, and Then,—the Present and To be,—
The Present seen,—the Future, God's decree,—
Blended their voices in sweet harmony.

" Before the Sun the Day-star!   Ere the Lord
His dread yet lowly mission shall fulfil,
One other Prophet's pleading shall be heard,
One other voice, in tenderest tone, instil
Love universal, heart to heart inclining;—
Meet greeting for the heavenly light's new
    shining.
Suddenly Christ shall in His temple stand—
Christ, whom ye seek!   His way before His face
Sent to prepare, last of the Prophet band,
A messenger shall tell His matchless grace,

THE ADVENT.

Clothed with Elijah's stern prophetic power,
Each listening heart grow ready at His word,
Children and Fathers hail the golden hour,
And join to greet the advent of the Lord!"

Thus Malachi **had sung, and at the strain**
The hope of Israel revived again,
And waiting hearts beat high;
Yet centuries flew by,
And one by one they throbbed themselves **to rest,**
And eyes grew dim in dusty death, **unblest;**
While dimly through the vista of long years
The **vision of the latest Seer appears;**
And in the wailings of a captive host
The echoes of the Prophet's song are lost.

Lost? nay, not lost! the **raindrops are not lost**
When the refreshing shower **hath ceased to** fall,
Although the parchéd **earth hath drunk them all.**
Deep in some silent cave
They find **themselves a grave,**
Till hands **unseen** beckon their onward way
To **life and day,**

And then upspringing at the soft wind's singing,
A harvest blessing marks the streamlet's way.
So, deep in lowly hearts, the Prophet's promise lay.

Gabriel hath spoke its resurrection word,
" Behold the Herald of th' approaching Lord!"

Elizabeth hath gained her home once more!
Welcome the whisper of the waving Palm!
Welcome the purple vine that drapes her door!
Welcome the Summer Evening's holy calm!
And yon wide landscape blending into dream,
Yon murmuring of the incense-laden stream,
Have they not lent a colour and a song
To many a happy thought in days bygone?
And now, like dear and spirit-haunted things,
They share the joy the present hour brings;
And while she hides from hearts less kindly prone,
They mutely seem to make her bliss their own.
Ah, happy home! what means the golden light
That lingers on the long familiar scene?
Is it a smile from passing angel bright
Still glows in amber on the fluttering green,

THE ADVENT.

His radiant wings have **wakened** as they passed ?
What means this gladness in repose at last ?
This **full and** perfect joy that knows **no scope**
Unpromised or uncertain ?—this one Hope,
Once dead **and gone, now** raised again in **power**
To resurrection life, immortal evermore ?
Yet Hope no longer. Hope is an imperfect thing,
Like this our present life,—aye wearying to take wing
Into the Future. It was Faith **now, standing**
Upon the shining threshold of all Good,
Like an emancipated spirit **landing**
From perils on Time's dark **and surging flood,**
At Heaven's gates, entranced, when opening wide
Forth flows in dazzling streams the glory-tide

Hark ! on the quiet morning's stilly air
Vibrate the echoes **of** approaching feet,
Brushing anon in haste the flowerets fair,
Then treading softly and sedate, as beat
The motive heart-throbs to delight or **awe.**
Mary draws near ! **Mary** by **Angel hailed**
" Thrice blessed among women !" Mary crowned,
In this first blossom **of her** radiant youth,
With such high honour that her spirit quailed

THE ADVENT.

Beneath its weight, and prostrate on the ground
She questioned of the wondrous vision's truth.
Mary o'ershadowed by the Highest's power!
Mary descended from illustrious King,
Yet lowly born, called to a nobler dower
Than Israel's twelve-starred diadem could bring.
The Virgin Mother to whose arms were given
The Christ, her Saviour, and her Land's Desire,—
The World's Redeemer,—The Adored of Heaven;—
Who meekly said—" According to Thy word
So be it to the Handmaid of the Lord!"
      Mary was come
With her glad secret to her cousin's home.
She needed not to speak. It was all known.
A sudden inspiration from above
Filling Elizabeth with loyal love,
Prompted a regal greeting. " Whence to me
The Mother of my Lord my guest should be ?
Hail, blessed among women ! Blessed Faith !
It shall be even as the Angel saith !"
Then Mary's pent up joy burst forth in song,
That deathless song that lives in echoes still,
The sweet Judean breezes bore along
Through all the world ! A melody to fill

THE ADVENT.

All hearts with ecstasy, all eyes with light,
Make Earth a Heaven—and Heaven itself more bright.

Have we not listened, in the twilight hour
The birds of song grow silent, one by one,
Till from the deep repose of moonlit bower
Each note of melody at last is gone?
So in the church's twilight songs were heard
Songs of the morning coming to the Earth,—
Prophetic strains which earnest spirits stirred
With holy thoughts, and gave great hopes a birth.
But one by one, as night drew darker round,
Th' inspired choristers had ceased to sound.
'Tis now the hour of dawn! though yet no beam
Gilds the horizon with its distant gleam,—
And hark! one clear voice rings upon the night,
Unrivalled in its trills of pure delight!
It is the Nightingale, waked by the breeze
That rustles as it hastens on its way
T'unfurl Aurora's flag on flowers and trees,
And pave with purpling shades the path of day.

And thus, methinks, it was the dawn-song rang
O'er Judah's hills when saintly Mary sang

THE ADVENT.

Time's mighty Anthem, on one voice alone,
While Heaven and Earth hung raptured on the tone.
Scarce had its thrilling music died away,
When lo! the Herald of the coming day!
The Angel-promised infant John is born,
And Israel hails the Day-star Prophet's dawn.

The Preparation.

"He was in the deserts till the day of his shewing unto Israel."

Luke i. 80.

The Preparation.

ABOVE, around, the golden sunshine reigns
    Oppressive, like a splendid tyranny,
    Upon a silent land where barren plains,
And white-teethed rocks, that gnaw with hungry edge
Th' horizon's dented line of cloudless blue,
Lie prostrate far and wide.
Still deeper than the sky in azure hue,
The Dead Sea heaves its hushed and noxious tide,
Unfringed with aught of verdure.
                      'Tis a sight
As desolate as Death itself, denied
Even a grave by still surviving spite
And hatred unappeased.

　　　　　　　　　　　In other lands
The sun looks kindly on the dewy earth,
And decks with waving forests shady strands,
And gives a thousand scented flow'rets birth,
And fills **the air** with many-tinted wings,
Weaving fair homes for beauty and for love,
Till day and night, **rejoicing** Nature rings
With songs **of praise to the great God above.**

But not so here, alas! **The** tyrant **Sun**
Scatters no blessing **from** his royal **hand,**
Only his burnished chariots **as** they **run**
Scar with long furrows all the panting land.

Deep in a rocky cradle sleeps the Sea,
A sleep of sullen dreams. No joyous thing
Its fair reflection hovers to behold
Upon its bosom, with a light-poised wing.
Among its visions, if a change there be,
'Tis but an imaged cloud, whose glooms enfold
Token of brooding storm.
　　　　　　　　　　Above, around,
Only the drone of the winged locust's way,

THE PREPARATION

Or murmurs of a laden Bee astray,
Rouses the slumb'rous air to life or sound.
Such is the desert! E'en the hungry flocks
Of Nomad Shepherd never wander here,
No pasture tempts a noonday halting near
The parched bare shadow of its crackling rocks.

Yet in this wildest spot of God's domain
He hath one living Temple; such as first
Th' Almighty placed in Eden's fruitful plain,
And breathed upon, and called th' enshrinéd breath
A human Soul. No fear of lonely Death,
Still less of gnawing hunger pangs, or thirst,
Could stay his path whom mighty thoughts impel
Awhile in dreariest solitude to dwell.

Strange choice for one so youthful, and endowed
With all most prized among the meaner crowd,
That once had passed him much admiring by.
A thousand rays of kindly feeling glanced,
Like star-fires, from the midnight of his eye,
Where Thought was throned, as 'neath a palace dome,
While to the wind her royal standards danced
Afloat to mark him for her chosen home.

THE PREPARATION.

Thrilled, too, from every iron sinew's length
The tokens of an all unwonted strength.
So formed to win the victor's envied place,
Strange thus, in starting, to decline the race;
To shun the peopled thoroughfares of men
And dwell apart, the desert's denizen.

Not with the languor of the weary, he
Had stepped into the by-way quietude,
Nor as the disappointed, to be free
Among the spectres of the Past to brood.

There are—but he was not of these—who blow
Some spark of their own kindling to a flame,
Intent alone upon its spiry glow;
Nor heeding other warmth, and other light,
Make it their Idol, but withhold the name;
Nor note that silently its vapours rise
To canopy their god, and build of night
A shrine
Which intercepts the beams divine
That fain would reach them from the upper skies.
One stern rebuke is spoken from the height,
And, swift as die the lightning's arrowy fires,

THE PREPARATION.

Their cherished flame, with flickering throe, expires.
Netted within the baffling folds of night,
They live, the victims of a blighted Past.
A desert home contents a desert heart,
Nor having lost a false god, seek the True.

Ah, John was not of these. A holier spell
Constrained him thus in solitude to dwell.

On Judah's hills, amid wild fern and flowers,
Stood the dear home where passed his childhood's
    hours.
No infant brother shared his slumbers calm
In the fond circling of his mother's arm.
No youthful radiance on her face he saw
Reflect in laughing light his dimpled mirth:
His earliest memories were tinged with awe.
Ever the Angel's shadow from his birth
Lingered around his footsteps, on his heart,
Till his young life became a thing apart.

With grave and matron grace, sedately sweet,
Elizabeth her child's appeal would meet,

And he was happy, not in noisy glee,
But in a calm and fruitful reverie.
Life's future work, to which his Parents' thought
Pointed with tender joy, was yet unknown.
Only he gathered from the things they taught
That Israel's God had marked him for His
　　　own;
And that a mighty mission would be given,
An embassage from the high court of Heaven.

Even in its mystery it had a charm
And training! Like a golden mist
Breathed from the lips of Summer morning calm,
Its beauty hid all meaner things, and kissed
Both Earth and Heaven, blending them to one.
And ever shed a dewy influence down,
That gave his fallow life, in time, a harvest crown.

At length a sorrow cast its chilling gloom
Athwart the sunlight of his childhood's home.
An Angel came
And stood by Zacharias as he prayed,
And called him by his name.
The summons was obeyed,

THE PREPARATION.

Upward the willing spirit fled!
The Priest was dead!

The mother and her son, in speechless woe,
Beheld the husband and the father go!
Yet Faith, in soothing tender accents, said—
" Be of good cheer; oh, weep not, but adore!
Often he went before
Leaving you praying in the outer court,
While he within the God of Israel sought;
And now before the bright celestial shrine,
He joins the church's worshipping divine;
From human frailty set for ever free,
He waits above, with wond'ring joy, to see
The great atoning off'ring which below
The Temple's ritual dimly did foreshow.
Be of good cheer, oh, weep not, but adore!
He is but passed a little while before,
Soon shall the Holiest's veil be drawn aside
And you ere long shall worship by his side."

Deepened the shadow on the mourning home,
Again the Angel, cypress-crown'd, was come.
Immortal life he to the Mother gave,
But left the Son beside a double grave.

THE PREPARATION.

A bitter pause! It seemed that life **stood** still
On one unechoed throb **of agony,**
And that **a dreary death-spell,** dark and chill,
A living soul in helpless trance had laid,
While close **at** hand there stood a haunting shade,
A black **Remembrance,** waiting but a breath
To torture life with pangs exceeding death.

Then John arose, and **with a Hero's heart**
He grappled with his **woe.**
He woke the black **Remembrance;** dared its dart,
Resolved the worst to know;
Gazed back on childhood's fleet and sun-winged hours,
Then left the peaceful home—the hallowed **grave,**
To loving eyes of stars, and birds, and flowers,
And, sorrow-braced, **his** purpose **waxed** more brave.
He looked into the Future, to discern
His destiny of duty, high and stern,
And then
Pledged it his life and faith **in** one sublime Amen.

In the wide world, so dim with quenchèd light,
He had no home, no rest!
Wander he might where other hearts were blest

THE PREPARATION.

With answering love, yet he was still alone.
If solitude whiles started at the tone
Of his heart's yearning, not to be repressed,
For human sympathy, the voice sped on
Unechoed, far beyond Earth's hoariest crest
Of purple mount, and cleft the golden sky,
And rang upon the battlements on high,
Till angel-sentinels returned salute
And kindly greeting, though the world was mute.

On! on! the vine-draped valleys had no charm
Could lure him to enjoy inglorious rest.
On! on! the Well by the o'ershadowing Palm
But nerved to further toil, when it refreshed.
The peaceful villages he journeyed through,
Marked him not come or go; his lonely way
Left record none, save that the stranger threw
A loving smile upon their babes at play.

Each day his childhood's home was distanced more,
And distanced, all of man;
And on the Dead Sea's line of dreary shore
The day-star Prophet's strange career began.

THE PREPARATION.

In solitude he wandered, thought-impelled,
Though thought was undefined,
Nor could its misty outline yet be spelled
In words or systems, to instruct mankind.
Therefore he wandered still, his noble soul
Chafing to carry tidings of great good
Through the wide world; yet checked by a control
So subtle that he doubted it was real—
So potent that it could not be withstood.

At times God gives the word,
And great the company who preach it round.
At times His voice is in His Temple heard,
But let the Earth keep silence at the sound.
Keep silence,—for no human tongue may frame
Meet language to enfold the thoughts Divine,
Nor Earth's sublimest euphonies find name
For all the glories of the Love and Light
Which from His Hiding-place burst forth and shine,
And in dread vision daze the Seer's sight.

This was John's time for silence, or such speech
As lost itself upon the desert air,
And died upon the distance, doomed to reach

THE PREPARATION.

No ear but His who hears Earth's every **voice,**
And in th' imperfect utterance could rejoice,
Even as a tender mother bends with care
To catch her Babe's first lisping of a thought,
And hails the voice with future meanings fraught.

This **was** John's time for training; in God's school,
With meek obedience, he must learn the law
Of the great kingdom whose one mightiest rule
Comprises all beside. With wond'ring **awe**
He deeper read the mystery,—" God is **One!**
And only to be worshipped!" " God is Light!"
And shines the universe's central Sun,
Enkindling every **ray** that greets **the sight**
With vision pure of Truth. All other gleams,
False, meteor-like, and quenched in early gloom,
That wander to mislead, are stolen beams,
Lurid with feeding **on the** brands of sin,
And flickering toward the darkness of the Tomb.
And " **God is** Love!" and must **be** loved
 supreme;
His gifts, in Him, and for His sake, must please,
And Self, the world's great Idol, bow its knees
In utter consecration **to** His will.

THE PREPARATION.

Alas! with every beam of Heavenly day
That through the Prophet's spirit sent its thrill,
The Shadow on the earth waxed deeper still!

How black the Fall looked, in that holy light!
To one who mused of God, how base was Man!
How mean was human greatness at its height!
How short was life, even at its longest span!
What halting progress Wisdom's stateliest stride!
What mimic—Pomp! and what delusion—Pride!

Far from his haunts Mankind may best be known!
The Babel of Earth's shouts, or wails, or songs,—
The wrestlings of its runners to the goal,
The phantom goal, to win a phantom prize,—
The lab'rinth footpaths of its busy throngs,—
Confuse the ears, and but mislead the eyes.
The more so that the echoes that are rife
Are not the sounds of only strife;
But loving whispers mingle there,
And joy thrills through th' elastic air,
And kindly greetings, claspéd hands,
Find place among the wand'ring Bands
That tread the road to Hell.

THE PREPARATION.

Nor is it darkness all.
For when the shadow of the Fall
Eclipsed the Sun of Righteousness, and fell
With blighting midnight on the race,
God in His pity left a starry train
To witness for Himself, and trace
A dim path upward to Himself again!
So dim that whether in the ages gone
A human spirit, by their light alone,
Climb'd ever up the height,
And e'en to Heav'n's Gate through the twilight
    stole,
And pleaded for God's alms to feed a soul
Hungry and thirsting, and then saw such light
Burst through the op'ning portal as revealed
A Friend within,
A substitute for sin,
We cannot tell, and God hath left concealed.

Far from Man's haunts the lonely John reviewed,
In bitter mem'ry, all the shame and wrong
With which the Highway of the Past lies strewed
By every Pilgrim of the busy throng
From Cain's time till the Present.

THE PREPARATION.

Then with strong
And passionate cries he wailed his fellows'
    crimes,
Sometimes in indignation; and sometimes
In pitying tears and agonizing prayer,
That woke strange echoes on the desert air.

Then followed silent sadness, when the glare
Of sunlight, so unvaried, seemed to mock
Unkindly all his load of darksome care,
And on the scarred face of each neighbouring
    rock
He read a taunt. Nor when a brooding cloud
Spread its grey shadow everywhere around,
And tinted with the colours of despair
The sullen tide-flow of the desert air,
Was that accordant; for, when his parch'd heart
Felt most of desolation, lo! a start
Of sudden joy rills from a hidden well!
And when the joy most sparkled he could tell
Of thirst unslaked, e'en by its clearest flow.
He needed sun and shade, for joy and woe
Chequered his onward path. Upon the earth
The netted shadows of the scanty grass

Spoke nearest sympathy. **All that hath birth,**
Whereon the sunbeams linger as they pass,
Hath underlying darkness!
                              Then awhile
A happier frame stole o'er him, and a dream;
A waking vision of his mother's smile,
Which, like a sparkling ripple set aflow
In childhood's early dawn so long ago,
Spread yet in wid'ning circles, till **the stream**
Of dreary life responded to the gleam;
And gave its Mariner a favouring tide
To duty and reward.
The magic of remembrance placed again
Old scenes around, when, childlike at her side,
He reverent joined the temple-seeking train,
Or gazed upon the quivering victim slain,
Whose blood proclaimed in every crimson stain
That sin is death, but not the sinner's death;
The panting substitute yields up its breath,
The guilty man goes free! Early he knew
The blood of meaner creatures could not do
The broken Law its reparation due.
They were but herald emblems of **the** grace
Which reconciles to God Man's fallen Race.

His mother's image brought another theme,
So woven with the temple, and with her,
That it came twinlike, **born of every dream**
In which **she lived.**
      He scarce knew what they were,
Those hidden **links whose** dim connexion bound
The Temple in its majesty profound
With one lone cradle in a cottage home!
The bleeding Lamb, the faint expiring cry,
With the most perfect type that Earth had known,
Or Heaven had loved, of Holy Infancy!
Mary's mysterious **Babe!** a household word
Around his Father's hearth! invoked as Lord
By those who never worshipped less than God!
What transports of thanksgiving at His name!
What storied lore of Portents when he came!
Angels, with song that clove the flashing sky,
" Glory to **God, and** peace on Earth " to cry!
A star, forgetful 'mong its peers to shine,
To pay a pilgrim visit at his shrine!

How oft of old, in holy Sabbath-tide,
His parents spake together, and to God,
Of Jesus, while he nestled by their side

THE PREPARATION.

And craved again the tales they **loved so well,**
He wond'ringly to listen,—they **to tell.**
How almost awful in its rapt delight
His Father's aged face! What tears and smiles,
Like sun and shower, wove **a** rainbow light
To deck her stories, when his Mother whiles
Took up **the sacred theme!**
      Then, on their boy
Fond gazing, thus they uttered forth their joy:—
" Thou, child, shalt be called
The prophet of the Highest, to proclaim
To souls by sin and darkness long enthralled,
Light and salvation in His blessed name!
Go to prepare the pathway **of** the Lord,
The dayspring that shall bid our darkness cease,
And, through the tender mercy of our God,
Shall guide our feet into the way of peace!"

How often as the hours flew by, beguiled
With saintly talk of Mary's holy **child,**
He eager pleaded, " Father, let me **go!**
I love Him, though unknown,—yet let **me know,**
That I may love Him more a thousand fold.
I, that am often wayward, would behold

His meek obedience, **that in** me may shine
Some fair reflection of His light divine.

" Oh, mother, mother,
I that have no brother,
I would **see Jesus**! He would be a friend
Such as **I sigh to** dream **of as I** wend
My lonely way among the browsing sheep,
Or in wild freedom climb the mountain steep.
I would attend Him lovingly,
Would watch each motion of His patient eye,
Would guard Him sleeping, solace when awake,
And grudge nor toil nor suff'ring for His sake."

Year after year, the yearning of his heart
Grew stronger to see Jesus. Yet apart
Their childhood passed, for God's time had not come.
Not as the dear companion of his home,
The day-star prophet must behold his Lord;
But as Messiah, to His Israel **sent,**
Crowned by the dove-like Spirit's bright descent.

Day after day, and year that followed year,
Found the lone Prophet in the Desert **drear;**

THE PREPARATION.

At times bewildered by excess **of** light,
As he gazed Heavenward ; or deep plunged in night,
As Earth, with all her darkness, mocked **his sight.**
Only when musing of the Holy One,
Man's sinless **Brother,** God's beloved Son,
Was Heaven's effulgence tempered to his eye,
Or Earth illumed with daylight from on high.
His life-long yearning stronger still became
To seek his Lord, and, having found, proclaim.

Day after day, by the blest Spirit taught,
He added golden links to chainéd thought,
Which, **craving** freedom, irked the Desert's bound
That barred him from his fellow-man around.
Nor did it err. The voice that seemed his own
Was only thus disguised. Not **from** His Throne
God thunders to His Sons. He whispers His behest ;
And rather, as they lay them down to rest,
A voice that seems but Eli's greets their ear,
Made only by its iteration known.
They **answer—**" Speak, Lord, **for** thy servants
    hear !"
When God to Israel spake, the voice was heard
Within the Temple's sacred courts, apart ;

THE PREPARATION.

And oft His children listen to the word,
Each in the quiet temple of **his heart.**

And solitude had done its work, and taught
Its lessons **well**; but at a costly price—
Long years of meditation! Life is short,
And meant **for action,** not for only thought;
And few are called on **for such sacrifice,**
Who yet are pupils in the school **of God.**
But here and there, **with great** endowments
　　graced,
Shines one above his fellows, therefore placed
In learning's higher paths, and rarely trod,
Apart to learn Salvation's deeper lore,—
Be disciplined to sterner rectitude,—
And thence **led outward to the world once more,**
Anointed teacher of its multitude.
Thus Moses learns two weary score of years,
Before as Israel's leader he appears;
Elijah thus for Ahab's presence trains,
In near communion with the King of kings,
Till human power he loftily disdains,
And scorns all fear, save such as loyal springs
Of error in the message that he brings.

THE PREPARATION.

Thus holy John,
Greater than all before
Of Woman **born,** his embassage must con
In lonely musings by the Dead Sea shore.

Solitude **is not** sanctity! they **err**
Who live apart, and deem they live for Heaven;
For **Man is** to his fellows given,
And in the tumult **and the stir**
Of **busy** throngs **must climb the upward way,**
Lending the fainting falling **ones a** hand
Of kindly succour;—guiding those who **stray**;
Sharing alike with **all** the pilgrim band
The storm **and** sunshine of **the narrow** way.

Uncalled by God, ah, Mortal! climb not thou
Presumptuous to the virgin mountain's brow
To crave a special audience, lest thy Lord
Be seeking thee upon the path below,
The beaten path of daily duty.—So
Thou miss the blessing He would fain bestow.
Thou hast thy reward!
Vain man looks up **with wonder to record**

THE PREPARATION.

Thy saintly height—then passes listless by,
Unblest in life, nor fitter made to die.

But when He calls thee, fear not to obey;
For He who knows the end must choose the way;
And be the desert howsoever drear,
A still small whisper shall rebuke thy fear,
"Thou art not quite alone, for God is here!"

When He speaks comfort, even Achor's vale
Becomes a door of Hope, whence songs arise
Heard in high Heaven, and echoed from the skies,
Till Earth wakes up to listen to the strain;—
"Thou art my people!" is proclaimed on High,
"And Thou my God!" that people's prompt reply.

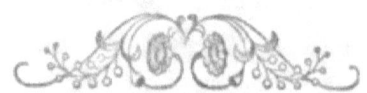

The Vocation.

"IN THOSE DAYS CAME JOHN THE BAPTIST, PREACHING IN THE WILDERNESS OF JUDEA, AND SAYING, REPENT YE, FOR THE KINGDOM OF HEAVEN IS AT HAND!"

Matt. iii. 1, 2.

The Vocation.

OBEDIENT to the Sculptor's high behest,
    Forth from the marble springs a human
        form ;
    With manly beauty every line imprest—
Each limb betokening power; while a storm
Of passionate ire flashes from the eye,
Or love shines tender, or despair appeals
In vain to silent Heaven. One passion, high
O'ermastering all the complex structure, wields
The sovereignty. The soulless block, upwrought
To the Ideal in some Human breast,
Is evermore th' exponent of a thought
It cannot share ;—inspired of love, or hate ;
Of Holiness, or Sin—of work or rest,
Through changes, changeless till the day of fate.

THE VOCATION.

All Paradise might light its beauty near,
Yet not a gloom disperse of sculptured woe;
Or Rama's anguish pierce the shivering air,
Yet 'bate no radiance from fair Psyche's glow.

Man carves the noblest form, but cannot breathe
The breath of life, or bid the bosom heave
With one responsive thought; while God endues
The meanest forms, the meadow's sparkling dews,
The fleecy cloudlet or the tangled weed,
With mute communion in the wanderer's need.
For God's works bear His Name sublime—"I Am;"
"I Am," Protean in its application
To all the wants of all His vast creation,
And more than lies in Time's horizon-scan,
Eternity His age—Infinitude His span.

He, the Great Spirit, not incarnate, dwells
Within the worlds He made,—wedded as soul
To body, He to Nature. Inspiration tells
Not He in it, but it in Him, "lives, moves,
And has its being." Under His control
The flowerets open, and the planets roll;
The glow-worm's lamp He kindles, and the Sun;

Small things are great, as parts of **a vast whole**,
Where, with one grand consent, one mighty Will is done;
Complexity and order; Harmony complete,
Through myriad diverse voices in the spheres.

Not only when the rill His Israel cheers,
Thirsting beneath the barren desert's heat,
Not only when the Manna's white-winged flake
Feeds mortal man upon the Angels' **bread**,
Doth He the pilgrim's weary **longing slake**.
For "not by bread alone shall man be **fed**,
But by his Maker's word,"
And rather felt **than heard**—
God speaking by the bright bird's joyous lay,
Or by the silent beauty of the **rose**,
A thousand subtle influences by day,
A thousand **mystic visions of** repose;
Not bearing tidings strange and new,
But calling into clearer view
The treasured memories hid asleep,
Of old, in the heart's castle keep.

The billowy years of conflict with strange thought,
And phantom gleams now blending into light,

THE VOCATION.

Precursive of th' embodied light of Heaven,
Were over; and the lonely Prophet sought
From other than the rifted rocks, and sight
Of sullen foam-fringe by the murmuring sea,
Communion with his mission destiny.
Slowly he journeyed, by this need impelled
To look for sympathy in softer scenes,
Where silvan creatures blythe their revels held,
And the grey desert died in leafy greens.

The wilderness is round him now !
Softly its zephyrs fan his brow;
He breathes the incense from the flower
Refreshed beneath the evening shower,
Where spiry columns bear on high
A leafy trellice whence the sky
Looks down benign, with starry eyes,
To watch the Prophet where he lies.
The dimmed air quivers with the wings
Of myriad lovely insect things;
The wild beast leaves his darksome lair,
And wanders stealthy through the wood,
With lustrous eye his prey to snare,
Or drink of Jordan's limpid flood.

THE VOCATION.

The river with its sparkling tide
Is ever on the onward glide,
And glittering forms of scaly life
Within its crystal depths are rife.
No lack of beauty all around,
No lack of wakeful **life or sound ;**
But in the wilderness **is found**
One only form of human kind,
Whom midnight folds beneath her wings,
And Angel guards **camp round to mind,—**
The envoy **of the King of kings!**

Thus through the silent watches lies
In slumber calm the Day-star Prophet, John,
Till black-winged night still further westward flies,
And morning dawns **the** leafy brakes upon.
Then in the **beauty of** young day's prime hours
Waking, he reverent kneels by some grey stone
Half peering from the woodland ferns and flowers,
And holds sublime communion.   Thus alone
In seeming only, for that prayer is **heard**
Through circling myriads narrowing to God's throne,
Each living star to star echoing the word

THE VOCATION.

Toward Heaven's central light;
And then exulting with supreme delight
That Need and Love are clasped in pure embrace,
And mortal sin hath met immortal grace.
Well they know,
Those Holy Ones that glow
Around the throne above,
That Blessings poised on outstretched wing
Hang ready at the beck of Love
To make the suppliant sing;
But judgments sleep
So still and deep,
They need a resurrection word,
Love's loudest tone,
To speed them to His own,
And if the falling of a tear be heard,
They linger on their way,
Pausing, lest God their dreaded mission stay
When His repentant children do but weep

While saintly John in prayerful ecstasy
Passed upwards through the blue gate of the sky,
And floated in the golden joys beyond,
Renewing thus in holy rest the bond

THE VOCATION.

That pledged his day to labour, there was found
New-waking life in all the hamlets **round.**
The toil of common handicraft again
Bid sinewy arm and ever-busy brain
Renew their avocations.   Rustic life
With rustic interests again was rife.
But something higher, something new, was there,
And musing silence marked the worker's **air.**
The Preacher of the Wilderness had **spoke,**
Unwonted light upon his darkness **broke,**
And **as** the Seer denounced **the doom of sin,**
That light disclosed its hideous form within!
As one who wakes from dreamed security
Beneath the crouching tiger's **glaring eye,**
So each had learned in terror that **he lay**
Within the grip of death a helpless prey!

When friend met friend upon the beaten **way**
To mutual **labour, and** the silence broke,
'Twas of the new Elijah that they **spoke ;**
For young and **old,** fair women and brave men,
Had heard the mighty Prophet in some glen
By Jordan's margin, and would hear again.

THE VOCATION.

Jerusalem was startled by his fame,
And crowds of wondering Pilgrims went and came
To see the lonely man whose stern rebuke,
Heard from afar, the royal city shook.
The haughty **soldier** of imperial Rome,
The silk-robed courtier from his palace-home,
The learned scribe, the cynic Sadducee,
All wended to the wilderness, where he,
Undaunted still, proclaimed in words of **fire**
The Advent of the long-foretold Messiah.

Hark! 'tis the murmur of a multitude
In these deep glades, so lately still and lone!
The hum of life! th' inseparable sound
Of numbers living, moving! Such a sound
As flows from wind-stirred leaves of forest trees,
As rises from the ocean's depths profound,
When " many waters " burden with their moan
The broad-spread pinions of the passing breeze.
A murmuring like a tide,
With rise and fall,
And inarticulate, for they speak **low**
Who speak at all.
At times so hushed its flow,

That the sweet silver river-song can **glide**—
Like heaven's cadence heard below
In earth's repose—
Upon the listening ear.
Yet not that Jordan **flows**
With **music in its ripple, are they** here
So hushed.   But that "the voice of one
That crieth in the wilderness" is heard!
And each would catch the first, the faintest tone
Of the new prophet's heaven-inspired **word.**

He—he alone attracts **th'** expectant gaze!
And now he rises!   Deeper still the **awe,**
Crouching in **silence,** 'mong the gathered crowd
That **wait his** thrilling words.   In bygone days
The Israelites **thus** greeted **Sinai's law**
From out the mountain's **black and vapoury shroud.**

Youthful he is—and **youth is beautiful!**
His locks **luxuriant, fit for** laurel **crown**
Of Poet or Hero!   But the furrowed frown
Beneath them speaks of **sterner** thought and things
Than Warrior seeks in battle, or than sings
The Minstrel to his lyre.

A leathern girdle clasps his vigorous form,
Braced by exposure to the Desert's storm.
And for his frugal fare
The locust and the wild bee's luscious store
Fulfil his scant desire :
He asks no more.

With outstretched hand, and clear and thrilling tone,
The Prince of Prophets makes his message known.

    "Thus, of old, Isaiah spake—
      Ere Messiah shall arise,
     Judah's Wilderness shall shake
      With the voice of one that cries—
    He is coming! promised long,
      Go ye forth your King to meet,
    Lay the paths, with shout and song,
      Straight for his victorious feet!
    For the Lord prepare a way
      Toward His temple dwelling-place!
    Hail the dawn of Israel's day!
      Bow before Messiah's face!

    " Hark! that voice is sounding now!
      Judah's wilderness resounds

With the tidings. Even now
   Ye who listen catch the sounds!
Pluck yon green boughs waving high;
   Rend the **air** with loud acclaim;
Say that Zion's King is nigh;
   Triumph in **Immanuel's** name!

" **No response!** What! silent all!
   'Tis the voice of Liberty
Taunts you with the Tyrant's thrall!
   Bids **you rise,** and make you **free!**
Not that ye are slaves of Rome
   Draws the hot tears from mine eyes!
Slaves **of** Lust! **I** weep your doom!
   Slaves of Lust! I bid you rise!

" **As I** wander deep in shade
   Of the woodland's tangled side,
Oft the glittering axe **is laid**
   At the root of forest pride.
Stroke by stroke the **echoes** mock,
   Moaning, swaying with each blow,
Till **at** last with thundering shock,
   Lo! the **sturdy oak** lies low!

THE VOCATION.

Fruitless trees, the axe is high,
 Wielded for your sudden doom,
Where the tree falls it shall lie,
 Hid in terror-haunted gloom!

"As I wander on the plain
 When the harvest-tide is o'er,
Gathered heaps of golden grain
 Plenteous strew the garner's floor;
But the chaff on rustling wing
 Flies before the winnower's breath,
Like a conscience-stricken thing,
 'Scaping from impending death.
Needed but some tiny sparks,
 And the red flames hiss on high,
Till a smoke-cloud only marks
 Where its smouldering ashes lie!
Where the World's ripe harvests stand,
 Mingles worthless chaff with grain,
But His fan is in His hand,
 Who shall judge betwixt the twain!
Fire that shall burn for ever!
 Rising smoke unquenchable!

Torment, intermitting never,
    Waits yon severed chaff in Hell!

"Brethren born of Abraham's seed,
    From your dream of safety wake;
They are Israelites indeed
    Who of Abraham's faith partake.
'Neath the ebon robes of Night
    Cowering sins are curtained close,
Vainly hid from human sight,
    God the guilty secret knows!
Tremble—for the day is nigh
    When the trumpet shall proclaim,
What a flash of His dread eye
    Drags to light of hidden shame.
Tremble, Sinner, and repent,
    Ere repentance be too late!
Ere the day of grace be spent,
    Ere the dreadful day of Fate!

"Bid the ploughshare of remorse
    O'er your souls its furrows drive,
Showers of tears bedew its course,
    Till its fallow wastes revive:

… Till God's golden seed dispersed,
 Falling on prepared ground,
Clothe **the world with beauty** first,
 And at length **Heaven's garners crown!**"

The Preacher paused, and scanned with anxious eye
The **swaying** tide of many human forms
Heaving and restless with awakening storms
Of new remorse.
     Out of the drowsy haze
Of years gone by dread spectres started forth;
And fettered consciences, like Samson, rose
To break the bonds of their betrayed repose:
Yea, rose invincible, in such fierce wrath
To vindicate their **power,**
That turned upon the conflicts of that hour
The issues **of** immortal destinies.

All this the Prophet knew
And marked he too,
With pitying tenderness, the rising sighs
That spoke surrender, and th' o'erflowing eyes
With **tears** of young repentance.
To his glance

The conflict now, portended coming peace;
The storm was wreathed in rainbow, and should cease,
To usher in deep calm and holy light,
Unstirred by tempest and unscathed by night.
Had he not bent
O'er a still lake, whose cradle, drap'd in flowers,
Was once a fissure in the mountain, rent
By dread volcanic powers?
A chaos once, the earthquake's ravage wild,
Where now the spangled meadow's verdure smiled?
And such he knew repentance, such the peace
That broods serene, when its wild conflicts cease,
And Heaven's love, as free as Heaven's rain,
That fills the well-springs of the thirsty plain,
Descends on desert souls with silver flow,
Adorning them with Eden's summer glow.

Lo! sudden as the arrowy lightnings start,
A new emotion filled the Prophet's heart,
Which kindled into ecstasy so bright
That who beheld were dazzled at the sight,
And held in wondering awe!
They saw not what he saw,

Although they also looked **toward Jordan's flood,**
By whose clear wave a **lonely wanderer stood.**

"**Behold the Lamb of God!**" the Prophet cries,
"**To darkling ash the Altar** fires may wane;
Behold the **all-sufficient sacrifice,**
Foreshadowed long by **lambs and** bullocks slain!
Said I not well, that **one among you stands**
Whom you know not?—so glorious and so great,
That mine, His Prophet's, are unworthy **hands**
To loose the sandals from His sacred **feet.**
This, this is He,
Who, coming after, **is preferred to me;**
E'en as the rising Sun casts into shade
The morn-star's herald rays, so I must fade
In the sweet dawning of you Heavenly Sun.
My task is well-nigh **done.**
I, **as** the Bridegroom's friend, proclaimed His
    Grace
And **Majesty, but now** behold **His Face!**
And woo'd and won **by** His attractive power,
I bid the happy Bride behold the Bridal hour!
Content to be forgot and silent, I rejoice
In the sweet accents of her Bridegroom's voice.

THE VOCATION.

"I knew Him not. But yester's dewy morn
There thronged to Baptism in Jordan's stream
Fresh groups of Pilgrims, weeping, sorrow-worn,
And sin-confessing; and among them came
One who confessed no sin, albeit, patient woe
Furrowed His gentle face. He wore a glow
Of mild compassion for His fellow-man,
And yet a majesty sublime, supreme,
As He surveyed with comprehending scan
The multitudes around His path that pressed.
Even, methought, as God Himself might scan
His six days' work, from out His Sabbath rest.

"I wist not what to say. The air around
Trembled with chords from every Prophet's
    lyre
To bear him witness, and the sunbeams danced
Like seraph messengers of living fire
Around His footsteps, as He calm advanced,
And bade me do mine office! Yet I stood
As one transfixed beside the river flood.

"Joy seized me, with the grip of sudden pain,
In the wild tumult, as the hot blood flashed

Athwart the throbbing chambers of my brain,
And left each pulse-gate quivering that it passed.

" As one awakened from a 'wildering **dream**
To sudden joy, when sense and memory seem
Fantastically one,
And both exact
A recognition from the faltering tongue,
So **I**,
Surprised, uncertain how to act,
Forbade Him baptism, scarce witting why.
Then, as the captain **of an** armed host,
Choosing **in thoughtless haste** a rallying post,
Not more secure than **many another near,**
Yet, having chosen, concentrates his skill
To **make the** stronghold worthy of its name,
And marshals all his legions round a hill
They must **defend, or bear a** traitor's shame,
Because he chose it—so I summoned round
Quick-gathered reasons to defend my ground
Beneath the charge of His rebuking eye.
' Lord! it **is I**,
I, who have need to be baptised of Thee,
And comest Thou to me?'

"Gracious He smiled a pardon, and replied,
'Yet suffer it to be so, for I came
Thus to fulfil the Law's remotest claim.'
Then I complied,
Following him, reverent, into Jordan's tide.
Mine heart forestalled the Heaven-promised sign,
I knew my Saviour, human and divine.
He filled the deepening void of weary years,
And love gushed forth in floods of happy tears.
For such a draught I thirsted on the wild
And desert plain, by hope alone beguiled.
And now, methought, the very fount of Heaven,
To quench that thirst, was to my parch'd lip given.
My childhood's lonely dream of human love,
A dream no longer, but a waking good!
My faltering prayers all answered from above—
Messiah's self beside His Herald stood!
I wondered not to see the Dove descend—
The sacred Dove, wherein the Spirit shone
In fluttering light, His Godlike path to tend,
Nor that the Father spake from His High Throne
To bear him witness, and bid Earth rejoice—
'This is My Son—My one beloved Son—
In whom I am well pleased. Hear ye his voice!'"

The Martyrdom.

"HE SENT AND BEHEADED JOHN IN THE PRISON."
Matt. xiv. 10.

The Martyrdom.

NCHALLENGED, up the marble
steps he trode,
That led to royal Herod's proud
abode.
The cringing sentinels, with cowering awe
Th' indignant Prophet's bold intrusion saw,
And hindered not his progress, as the clang
Of his swift footstep on its pavement rang.

And now along the corridors there stirred
The balmy fragrance of some rare perfume,
A breath of Araby, the maiden bloom
Of prisoned flowers, escaping silently.
Sweet distant music, dream-like, too, was heard;
The whisper of some pleading melody,

That seemed to woo them in their secret flight,
And bid them back to beauty and delight.
"The world without is chill,
And ye would die,
Dear fragrances, upon the evening air!
Oh, linger still!
And on the zephyrs lie,
That softly float around the royal pair."

Nearer the kingly presence now
John drew, nor faltered when the gauze-dimmed
    rays
Of starry lamps broke on his eager gaze;
Nor when he dashed aside, with sudden fling,
The spangled veil, and stood before the king,
With scathing scorn-flash on his frowning brow.

Aback the courtiers started, stricken dumb
With blank amazement.—Who was this had come
Unbidden, like a spectre of th' abyss,
T' unmask a vision of forbidden bliss,
And make it vanish like a bubble, blown
And burst? Yet none dare give his wonder tone
While Herod trembled silent on the Throne.

THE MARTYRDOM.

At last John spoke,
And like the first dread thunder-stroke,
Upon the mute assemblage, terrible
The Prophet's message broke.

Turning, he pointed where the Queen reclined,
Unmindful of her form's voluptuous grace—
Unmoved to pity by her pallid face,
And quivering lips, and eyes with terror blind,
And bosom heaving with the conflict wild
Of jarring thoughts bestirred to mortal strife.
"Thou may'st not have her! She thy Brother's
  wife!
It is not lawful!"

            While in distance lowers
The black-brow'd tempest crouching for its spring
To devastate the Earth, all Nature cowers
In dreadful hush; no sound of living thing
Breaking the truce, or rising up to dare
The battle shock, or haste the impending blow.
But once the thunder rushing through the air,
Inflicts on struggling Earth her anguish throe,

Then she starts up with wild defiant strength
And cry of conflict. The rebuke at length
Had passed the Prophet's lips, and broke the spell
That erst upon the appalled assembly fell.

Herodias rose! most like the crested snake,
A beauty and a loathing! Thus she spake,
Her sharp tongue loosed to dart its arrowy spite
Of poisoned malice—

" Talk to slaves of Law!
Here Will is Law! and only serfs obey
The Will imposed by others!
Lust is Law, if Lust and Might are brothers!
Say thy nay
Where bonds and stripes enforce thy mandates stern;
We, with the laugh of scorn, thyself and message
 spurn.
We spurn thee! bid thee from our presence forth,
Yet not without thy guerdon, for our wrath
Is just, oh Martyr-seer, therefore go
To all the glory of the Martyr's woe:
The Martyr's crown,—let Him who sent bestow!
On every wrinkle of thy quivering face
We'll write a tale of anguish and disgrace;

And each deep line a new demand **shall** bring
Against the justice of high Heaven's King.
Thy crippled limbs, thy darkened orbs of sight,
Thy lone years wasted in the dungeon's night,
Shall doubtless **each such** lib'ral largesse gain,
As well **shall** compensate for present pain!"

Calmly the Prophet stood ; **her vengeful word
Hearing** with almost **pity, for he knew
An** Angel with averted visage heard
Her impious **threat'nings too,**
Seated amid the **Archiv'ry of Heaven,**
To whom the inexorable task **was given**
To register men's **crimes!**

She waved **her hand,**
And at the mute command,
Around his wrist
The cold remorseless manacles they twist,
Filching his freedom.   Yet he scarcely **felt**
Their pressure, for his thoughts the rather dwelt
Upon his errand.   **Had it been** fulfilled
As God who gave the martyr-mission willed ?

Then should his further service lie
In prison;—he was prompt to bear
His witness to the truth e'en there—
In death—he was resigned to die!

This was the language of his inmost soul,
And silently it rose, as good thoughts rise
Like waters to the level of their fount,
And Angels heard it in God's Holy Mount;
For is not Heaven the cradle and the goal
Of all that here is pure, or strong, or wise?

They led him from the Palace warmth and light
In fetters, through the early-gathered night,
Not yet so dark but that the busy throng
Knew him, and wondered, as he passed along.
The breath of evening played upon his brow,
His burning brow, like friendship's gentle kiss,
Thus had it soothed his weary soul ere now,
Amid the conflicts of the wilderness.
With head bowed down, and silent, passed he by
Those streets so long familiar to his eye—
Those homes that knew him as an honour'd guest—
Those friends beloved that round his footpath pressed—

Their kindly greeting lost upon his ear
That dared his Guards, and bade him be of cheer.

He gave them all no heed,
Abstracted still, he passed them by,
For God who knew His Servant's need
Was breathing solace from on high;
And as God's light
Banishes earthly objects into night,
And makes the universe a temple wide,
Where He alone is seen and glorified,—
So when His voice is heard
Communing with His honoured creature, man,
There needs no Herald Angel's word
Commanding silence; there may rage around
Earth's Babel cries, and yet the listening ear,
Enraptured with His voice, in all th' extended sphere
Will catch no other sound.

Nor more he heeded, when the prison gate
Creak'd on its iron hinge, a captive's fate,
Proclaiming with a dull and echoing groan
To other captives, weeping for their own.

THE MARTYRDOM.

A narrow cell
They gave him where to **dwell**,
The mem'ry of the **Past** for company,
For even **Hope grew** languid at his side,
Till silently **it died.**

Slowly and sadly, 'neath Life's leaden skies,
The hours passed, their drench'd wings could not rise,
So wet with tears, so chill with wintry sighs.
Day stole upon him **like the** pallid **ghost**
Of an unresting night,
And midnight's **wand** invoked a ghastly **host**
Of spectre forms that mocked his **straining sight.**

What wonder **that, the martyr aid withdrawn**
Which nerved **to** daring **deed,**
John's lion-heart grew faint, as all forlorn
He felt a deeper need :
A higher service, sacrifice **more pure,**
God now required,—the Patience to endure !

When God would limn the portrait of His Church
In pilgrim garb, all principalities
And Powers of Heaven draw near in glad surprise,

His Wisdom manifold intent to trace
In every complex line.   Grace after grace
Adorns the sketch, revealing clearer trace
Of Christ her elder brother.   " Oh how fair!"
With rapture cry the Holy Watchers there ;
" 'Tis the King's daughter, robed in spotless white,
With   Heaven's joy sparkling in her eyes' soft
    light!"

While yet they gaze, to peace that joy He tones!
And fairer, purer still, each Seraph owns
The marvellous portrayal!   " Surely now
Beauty ineffable adorns her brow."

Another change
They watch, and passing strange !
Even the Peace hath faded from the face,
And dim-eyed sorrow hath supplied its place ;
Till Patience kindles there a holy smile,
Reflection from a sacrificial fire
On her heart's Altar.   " Perfect and entire
The beauty now !" each wond'ring Angel cries ;
And " Wanting nothing !" God Himself replies !

THE MARTYRDOM.

Yea, Patience is the crowning beauty, given
The nearest to the opening gate of Heaven!
Along the pathway various graces meet
The journeying Bride, the gifts of nuptial love.
But Patience is the bridal-wreath, above
The whole, and then she stands complete!

And what is Patience? Not submission only
To any fate, however dark and lonely.
Patience is silent Hope, with folded wing,
When it can neither fly nor sing,
Content to rest in darkness till its flight
Is beckoned forth,—but gazing into light
Of future joy, by that alone sustained,
Till all its glorious heritage is gained.

Oh, hardest lesson, slowly learned below
In every varied phase of mortal woe!
Its type the rainbow's arc, a jewelled form
Set in the background of a dark'ning storm,
Yet born of light clear shining far away,—
The child of darkness, wedded unto day!
Not less a type, because when storms are gone
A rainbow shines around th' Eternal's Throne.

For deem'st thou Patience mortal? Nought is so
Of good; nor doomed to find below
Its final mission. Christ, who most possessed
The lovely grace, hath borne it to His rest,—
" Henceforth expecting!" Patience waits in gladness
For more of joy from out the Future's store,
As truly as she waits, resigned in sadness,
Till sadness be no more.
'Tis Patience keeps the time
For all Heaven's choral symphonies sublime,
Which else were discord.

                Now a drearier woe,
The last and darkest, drenched the Prophet's heart.
He was resigned that all of Earth should go,
Yea, life itself depart;
But not that the Messiah should forsake
His fainting servant, captive for His sake.
One word of sweet approval from His tongue,—
One token of His sympathy and care,—
And joy once more exultingly had sprung
To bless his gloomy Prison of Despair.
Day after day he listened for that word—
Night after night—but never, never heard!

Thousands were daily thronging to His side,
As now he taught by Galilean tide,
And none who craved a blessing were denied.
Yet when John's **friends** the wond'rous tidings
   brought
Of **Heavenly mysteries** Messiah taught,
He **eager** questioned, " Does He think of **me?**"
They answered, " Nay!"—they answered pityingly;
And all the anguish which that answer gave
They know who for one **love, and but one, crave**
In vain.

Love speaks in parables throughout the world.
In Heaven, perchance, its messages are known
By the **mute** glisten of **an** answering eye.
But here it shrinks abashed to hear the **tone**
Of its own voice, and gives itself the **lie**
When craving credence most. The realest thing
Below the sapphire sky,
Exorcised with a grasp, and vanishing!
Eluding with a swift ethereal wing
Each fettering hand, seems like **a** maiden's dream
Most insubstantial!

E'en the opal's gleam
Is not so changeful in its colouring!
Now cold as emerald in its springtide green;
Then flushing with the ruby's burning ray;
Paling to pearl,—anon Heav'n-tinted seen
Like the blue palace of a summer day!

As self-forgetful as a mother's smiles
When her soft lullaby her child beguiles
To slumber, Love appeareth whiles:
Wounded anon by an averted look,
Or sympathy expected and denied,
It wears the mask of all-unlovely Pride;
Yet weeps hot teardrops quenchless from its eyes
To find itself mistook
Behind its strange disguise.

And now John's Love must speak,
Or else his long o'erburdened heart must break—
Must speak to earn reply,
Or of his lov'd One's silence droop and die.
Yet asked he not what most he craved to hear,
Lord, dost Thou love me?—Dost Thou think of me?

And is my lost life, in the dungeon drear,
A sacrifice acceptable to Thee?

They must be gifts, not alms,
Love's jewelled words for memory's treasury;
When asked for, losing half their charms!

Nor would he sow in other breasts the fear
That Jesus ceased to hold His servant dear,
Which yet perplexed his own. Could he have gone
Himself to seek Him, one sweet smile alone
Were all the proof he needed.

       But he sent
Two of his friends to ask,—as if intent
Only to seal his mission with the proof
Of Christ's Messiahship, "Tell us in truth,
Art Thou indeed the Saviour promised long,
Or look we for another?" Hid among
The questioning words, there lurk'd an anguish-cry,
Scarce audible, so deep the misery
From which it came,—" Dost Thou remember me?"
It reached Christ's ear; it brought a prompt reply,
And worthy of His lofty courtesy.

He lavished works of wonder all around;
The sick were heal'd; the blind their sight received;
The lame man walk'd; deaf ears unclosed to sound;
The hardened **wept;** the weeping poor believed!

"Tell John," Christ said, "what ye have seen and
    heard,
The power divine **of** My transforming word!
And blessed shall My servant **be**
Who findeth no offence in Me!"

Such was the message, such the stern **rebuke**
The awed disciples **to their** master took.
But John **a secret** message found
Conceal'd in this of harsher **sound,—**
"In these **my works** acknowledge **Me!**
Such as thou hear'st to these **I be,**
Such will I prove Myself to thee!"

Dim in the distance disappeared the forms
Of John's disciples, followed by the eye
Of Jesus, blessed perchance unconsciously,—
The blessing welcomed, but the source unknown,
A royal largesse from a hidden throne.

Then Jesus turned Him to the crowd again
To vindicate His suffering servant's fame.
" What went ye to the wilderness to see?
By Jordan's banks, what strange attraction drew
Your list'ning crowds? The shaken reeds that
    grew
Beside the water, breathing melody?
Æolian lutes on which the zephyrs played,
Filling with song each cool and tranquil glade?
What went ye to the wilderness to see?
A courtier decked in silken bravery,
Dispensing favours? Nay, ye such had sought
Within the confines of the Royal court!
What went ye to the wilderness to see?
A Prophet? Yea! and more, for this is he
Of whom Isaiah spake long ages past,
Of woman-born the greatest and the last!
Great were the Seers who bade their nation
    hope
For blessings that far future years would bring,
But ah, his message hath a nobler scope,
Whose sudden voice
Bids the wide world rejoice,—
The time is come! Behold the promised King!

THE MARTYRDOM.

Great is my Herald! He is greater still
Who owns my sway, and yields him to my will!
What tho' John's voice is mute, tho' lonely woe
Consume his captive hours as they flow,
What tho' forgotten by the crowd that hung
Enraptured once on his prophetic tongue,
They hold him greater in his suffering love,
Who watch him from the kingdom gates above,
Than when, with stern Elijah's power arrayed,
The spirits of the multitude he swayed.
Yea, greater than the greatest Prophet he,
Accounted least of those that follow Me.
More eloquent my martyr-servant's sigh
Than rapt Isaiah's grandest prophecy!"

Light twinkling feet in Herod's sparkling hall
Greet their reflection in the polished floor,
Swift as the dripping swallow's pinions fall
To wake the slumb'rous wave he hovers o'er.
Lost in the whirl of dance, a lovely mist
Of merry stars, afloat in rainbow cloud,
Herodias' daughter keeps the court a-whist
In admiration! There is heard no sound,

Save such as holds the measure of her dance,
Nor listless wanders e'en an errant glance;
Unmindful of her beauty's magic glow,
She lingers now, and lo! her slack'ning pace
Heightens the charm of her enthralling grace,
As faultless in repose,
As in the hazy outline, which her speed
Had thrown around her! Even so, the rose
Starts from her morning veil of golden beams,
Or blushing fruit in mellow ripeness gleams
From the green shelter of its wind-stirred leaves.

One glance around the royal damsel gives,
Elate the guerdon of her skill to see
In the mute homage of each glowing eye;
Then soft she drops upon her bended knee
Before the king, "Ah, deign, Great Majesty,
A token of thy favour to bestow,—
Some opening flower to bloom upon my breast,
And, with its fragrant breathing, whisper low
That thou art pleased!" To whom the king replied,
"Ask what thou wilt, it shall not be denied,
Though half my realm were in the bold request!"

THE MARTYRDOM.

The courtiers listened, wond'ring what a maid
   So gifted, young, and beautiful would crave.
But still she paused as though she were afraid
   To unmask her wish, or as her heart misgave
The royal word, on which perchance there hung
A hope too sacred for her trembling tongue.
Thus Herod judged, and bending from his throne,
" Sweet Princess!" said, " make but thy wishes known,
And, by the guests that honour us to-day,
Ask what thou wilt, I will not say thee Nay!"

Thus urged, and in her Mother's cruel eye
Reading anew her pre-arranged reply,
The fair girl said,—
" Here, in a charger, John the Baptist's head!"

Cold horror seized and silenced all the host
Of startled courtiers, and the 'wildered king—
Trembling and pale, as though the Prophet's ghost
Already hovered on revengeful wing
To bear the tidings of such murder fell
Through the wide world,—with hoarse and quick-
    drawn breath,
As left in madness to some demon's spell,
Gave sentence for his death!

THE MARTYRDOM.

He turned him not, e'en at Herodias' touch,
That would recall him **to a calmer frame,**
Such as the festive scenes around became.
His frozen eyes refused to quit their clutch
Of his **false** temptress, as he feared some art
Of the black devil crouched within her heart,
Should waft her to **some trackless desert** forth,
Leaving him lonely to th' avenger's **wrath.**

The lamps burned dim; the guests with stealthy tread
Stole from the **haunted gloom**
Solemnly, as one quits an honour'd tomb,
And in the **ebon sky,**
With golden stars' funereal 'broidery,
Beheld the Pall which God Himself had spread
Above the form of the illustrious **Dead.**

The lamps burned out, where yet the royal Three,
Bound by the new-forged fetters of their sin,
In silent **conclave, chill** with misery,
Feared the wild spectres, starting from the dim
Shadows of night;
Yet dared not stir to light
One quenchéd **lamp,** of all that hung around.

THE MARTYRDOM.

But see! along the ground
A streak of red!
Cleaving the darkness with a stroke as dread
As of the sword which 'fended Eden round.
Beneath the portal of the Hall it flashed,
While nearing, through the corridor there crashed
The heavy footsteps of two blood-stained men,
Bearing a ghastly trophy! Shuddering then,
Herodias' daughter, with averted face,
Took the grim meed of beauty and of grace,
And bore it to her mother!

              There it lay,
In ruddy halo of a martyr's blood,
A noble head, and youthful, for its day
Of life still clomb aloft to golden noon,
When all too soon
The murderer's axe benighted it in death!

Herodias gazed with quicker coming breath;
And through the vista of all future years
That look
With stern rebuke

Still met her eye.
She saw it horrified, until her fears
At times grew audible in sudden cry,
" 'Tis John whom Herod murdered!"   "Nay," they said,
The shocked attendants, " Nay, for John is dead!"
To whom Herodias, frantic would reply,
" He is not dead!   The murdered never die!
A million Johns sprang from his gaping throat
With starting eyes that on my misery gloat,
In whose cold hands a million lightnings hiss
My weary soul to Hell!
Is he in bliss,
Sped thither by the sudden stroke that fell
Athwart the iron chain of captive life
That bound his soul to misery and strife?
Why should he thus revenge a fate so blest?
Can he not slumber in his grave of rest?
Art thou not he?   Phantom, thy name I ask?
Is it not John?   That gory head I know
Some mocking demon wears it as a mask,
For it was dead!   Yea, in his form a-dressed
Some cruel Spirit goads me to my woe
The other side of Death!

THE MARTYRDOM.

"The Palace Halls
Are terrible with 'Mene' on the walls,
And every voice takes up the curst refrain,
And echoes 'Mene' through my maddened brain!"

Without the dungeon gate
A band of grief-bowed pilgrims wait;
Not weeping as they weep
Whose loved one, waking from a holy sleep,
Hath waked above;
But petrified with horror and amaze
At tidings of a bloody Martyrdom,
Into the others' pallid faces gaze,
Each craving contradiction of his fears.
They come
In all the stony weight of sudden woe
That cannot melt in flow of hallowed tears;
Yet half-incredulous,—the treacherous blow
So unexpected fell which killed their joy,
That Hope, in terror fainting, could not flee,
But lingered, murmuring still, "It cannot be!"

A jailor came,
Guarding with blood-stained hand the shuddering flame

THE MARTYRDOM.

That led them to the corpse. The night's black wind
Went with them by the open iron gate,
And followed through the dismal passages,
Moaning and sighing for the Prophet's fate.

'Tis all too true!
In the deserted cell the headless trunk they view
With reverent awe, that still restrains their cries.
The roofless temple there in ruin lies,
Of a transcendent soul!

                            In fear they stood,
Still musing on the recent deed of blood,
Which to their fancy took a form of dread,
Haunting the glooms around; for it is said
The Fiend who tempts a murderer to his crime,
Is henceforth prisoned in some human shape
Bearing a hideous likeness to the Dead,
From which the captive demon may not scape,
Through all the cycles of all coming time!

They took the Body up;
Smoothing the stiff'ning limbs with pious love,
Contorted still with that last mortal throe

Which sped the spirit to its home above.
They bore it with a slow
And solemn dirge along the echoing way
By which they came,
Needing no more the flame
Of flickering torch, their mournful path to show,
For now the silver beams of dawning day
Were lighting up the dungeon's gloomy vaults
With early grey.

   "Sadly we bear thee forth
    In the lone tomb to dwell,
    Victim of royal wrath;
      Brother, farewell!

   "Up to high Heaven's gate,—
    Down to Death's narrow cell,
    Driven with cruel hate;
      Brother, farewell!

   "Oh, the sharp agony,
    When the keen weapon fell,
    Setting thy Spirit free!
      Brother, farewell!

THE MARTYRDOM.

" Oh, the wild terror-pang
  When through the dungeon cell
  Murderous voices rang!
    Brother, farewell!

" Last of the Prophet line!
  Who shall thine honours tell?
  Herald of Light divine!
    Brother, farewell!

" Israel's Morning Star!
  Upward our voices swell
  Borne to thy home afar!
    Brother, farewell!"

And now the sad procession wound its way
Adown the rocks on which the city stood,
And at their feet green meadows stretched away
In flowery slope toward Jordan's rippling flood.
They dug a grave, deep in a leafy dell,
And once again they wail'd a long farewell.

The glorious Sun had drawn his curtains back,
Of purple clouds, pavilioning his rest,

And golden glory paved his Sovereign track
Toward the far chambers of the fragrant west.

He lit a halo round the Prophet's bed
Of calm repose, and on the mourners shed
His gifts of light and hope, leading them on,
No more forlorn,
To where, even now, in Heaven's radiant morn,
The Day-star Prophet shone!

Thus shall the Sun of Righteousness arise
With healing wings, a weary world to cheer!
The Day-star pales upon th' illumined skies!
The Herald falls! the King Himself draws near!

Celestial visions that around them burned
Inspired their lips as homeward they returned.
They communed of the open pearly gate,
At whose pure portals choirs of Angels wait,
Calling in trancing song across the tide
Of sapphire space on which freed spirits glide;
By melody the Blest may only hear
Guiding their journey to their own bright sphere!
They communed of a river of delight,
Whose radiant source no Angel's eye hath known,

Lost in infinitude of awful light,
Proceeding from th' Eternal's dazzling Throne!
Of draughts of immortality! Of life
Exulting ever in unfading youth!
Of knowledge gazing on the wonders rife
In all the vast transparencies of Truth!
Of tenderest Friendships fearing no farewell!
Of noble deeds attuned to harps of gold!
Of jewelled crowns for Holy Ones who dwell
In crystal towers of rich celestial mould!
They called it Heaven! They said that God was there!
His Smile the Light that thrilled yon world above!
His Will the Service Saints and Angels share
With all the sweet alacrity of Love!

Hush! words were traitors to the thoughts that
    glowed
In vision of the Prophet's bright abode!
And vision failed before the amber Throne!
The mysteries of Heaven are only known
Transfigured into Symbol!

THE END.

www.ingramcontent.com/pod-product-compliance
Lightning Source LLC
Chambersburg PA
CBHW022146160426
43197CB00009B/1453

*9 7 8 3 3 3 7 0 2 8 3 1 2 *